12-12

DATE DUE		
JAN 1 8 2013		
APR 1 1 2013		

J.K.
ROWLING

Essential Lives

J.K. ROWLING

EXTRAORDINARY AUTHOR

by Victoria Peterson-Hilleque

Content Consultant:
Edmund M. Kern, PhD, Professor of History
Lawrence University, Appleton, Wisconsin

ABDO
Publishing Company

8/17
34 22

CREDITS

Published by ABDO Publishing Company, 8000 West 78th Street,
Edina, Minnesota 55439. Copyright © 2011 by Abdo Consulting
Group, Inc. International copyrights reserved in all countries. No
part of this book may be reproduced in any form without written
permission from the publisher. The Essential Library™ is a
trademark and logo of ABDO Publishing Company.

Printed in the United States of America,
North Mankato, Minnesota
052010
092010

Editor: Holly Saari
Copy Editor: Michele Simms-Burton
Interior Design and Production: Kazuko Collins
Cover Design: Kazuko Collins

Library of Congress Cataloging-in-Publication Data
Peterson-Hilleque, Victoria, 1971-
 J.K. Rowling, extraordinary author / by Victoria Peterson-
Hilleque.
    p. cm. — (Essential lives)
 Includes bibliographical references and index.
 ISBN 978-1-61613-517-1
 1. Rowling, J. K—Juvenile literature. 2. Authors, English—
20th century—Biography—Juvenile literature. 3. Potter, Harry
(Fictitious character)—Juvenile literature. 4. Children's stories—
Authorship—Juvenile literature. I. Title.
 PR6068.O93Z824 2010
 823'.914—dc22
 [B]
                                    2010000503

J. K. Rowling

TABLE OF CONTENTS

Rowling wrote much of Harry Potter and the Philosopher's Stone *in cafes in Edinburgh, Scotland.*

WRITING THE FIRST BOOK

Joanne Rowling pushed her daughter in a stroller along the streets of Edinburgh, Scotland. She was on her way to a cafe to sip a cup of coffee and work on her book, which she had been writing for four years. It was 1994, and money was tight. Rowling could not find work that would support her and her child and pay day-care expenses. She was living on welfare, although she still worked as a secretary to supplement her state benefits. In her spare time, she followed her lifelong dream of becoming a writer.

Rowling had moved to Edinburgh one year before to be near her sister, Dianne. Recently separated from her husband, Rowling was looking for a fresh start after living and teaching English in Portugal. She believed Edinburgh would be a good place to raise her daughter, Jessica, and a good place to pursue a writing career. Rowling showed her sister the first few chapters of her book, and Dianne encouraged Joanne to keep writing.

An Informal Writing Studio

When Dianne's husband, Roger, opened Nicolson's Cafe in the early 1990s, it became like a writing studio

Impact on a Reader

The Harry Potter books have affected readers in many ways. One young fan commented on how the books opened her mind to understanding literature: "Until I read the Harry Potter books, it was only reading. I read fantasy, that was it. After reading the [Harry Potter] books, though, I turned into an author—a writer, I imagine. Now I scrutinize and analyze books. . . . It's a different way of looking at things, and it has made me better appreciate what authors do and the works they create. I can now reread books and appreciate their value in sparking children's imaginations all the more."[1]

for Rowling. Prior to writing in Nicolson's, she wrote in coffee shops, sometimes feeling self-conscious when she drank the same cup of coffee for hours. At Nicolson's, Rowling could relax and let her mind roam around the magical story she was creating. It was at this cafe where she developed the intricacies of her tale of the young boy who would capture the attention of so many readers—and a tale that would take her 17 years to complete.

Rowling was realistic about her prospects of becoming a writer. She was unknown and knew she would have trouble finding a publisher to give her work a chance. So Rowling took steps to become a teacher in Scotland, in case a writing career did not work. Even though she previously taught in Portugal, she needed to obtain a postgraduate certificate of education to qualify to teach in Scotland. The certificate required

Mistakes in the Series?

Despite Rowling's attention to details, close readers have pointed out mistakes in the Harry Potter series. In chapter nine of book seven, Hermione tells Harry and Ron she has never before used the obliviate spell to erase a person's memories. However, in chapter six she said she modified her parent's memories and hid them in Australia to keep them safe from Voldemort.

Rowling has disputed the claim that this is a mistake. She said modifying a person's memory is not the same as using the obliviate spell, which erases memories.

Although Rowling's dream was to become a published author, she could not foresee the tremendous success her debut book would have.

acceptance into a yearlong teaching preparation course. Joanne was accepted, and she received a grant from the Scottish Office of Education to support herself and Jessica while becoming a full-time student.

The Creation of a Future Phenomenon

Once accepted into the program, Rowling set the goal of completing her book before beginning school to obtain her teaching certificate. She knew the demands of preparing to be a teacher along with single parenting would not give her extra time to write. It was a daunting task, however. *Harry Potter and the Philosopher's Stone* (published as *Harry Potter and the Sorcerer's Stone* in the United States) was only the first of seven books in a series that Rowling had planned. Each book was meticulously

Careful Planning

Rowling had to plan her books very carefully because many details in each book would become important later in the series. She has said, "I almost always have complete histories for my characters. If I put all that detail in, each book would be the size of the *Encyclopædia Britannica*."[2]

For example, in book one, details are given that in later books show Harry's connection with Voldemort, Harry's enemy. As a baby, Harry received a lightning-shaped scar on his forehead after Voldemort tried to kill him. In book seven, it is revealed that when Voldemort tried to kill Harry as a baby, he left a piece of his soul in Harry. This event is foundational to the connection between Harry and Voldemort throughout the series. Ultimately, this allows Harry to survive when he defeats Voldemort.

When Harry picks out his wand in book one, he learns that it contains a tail feather from a phoenix who gave up another tail feather for only one other wand—the wand Voldemort used to try to kill Harry. However, it is not until book four that readers learn that wands that are "brothers," such as Harry's and Voldemort's, will not work properly when they fight against each other. This saves Harry's life when he duels with Voldemort in book four.

outlined. Rowling needed to plan the entire series before finishing the first book because details of plot and characters' lives could play a role in a future book. In a shoe box, she kept copious notes so she would not make mistakes.

In 1995, Rowling reached her goal. *Harry Potter and the Philosopher's Stone* had taken her nearly five years to finish—partially because of her life's events and partially because of the complexity of the work itself. Shortly after, a literary agency agreed to represent her and a publisher decided to publish the book.

Once published, *Harry Potter and the Philosopher's Stone* became a best seller. Children and adults eagerly read the book and waited expectantly for the next installment in the Harry Potter saga. Rowling busily worked on writing the rest of the story. With each book, the success of Harry Potter increased. The books won

Letters from Kids

In the collection *Kids' Letters to Harry Potter*, letters were compiled from young readers all over the world. The fans had addressed these messages to Harry Potter. In one letter a fan from the Philippines wrote to Harry, "Though you live in a world very foreign to me, I feel like I know you. Maybe I see myself in you. Not in magic, but I can relate to the way a growing kid manages to live through life's surprises."[3]

While the target audience for the books was young readers ages nine to 13, adults have also been captivated with the books. In Great Britain, special editions of the books have been released with different art on the cover that appeals more to adult readers.

awards and continued to be on bestseller lists. Parties were held for the release of each book, and the books were made into popular movies. Harry Potter merchandise lined the shelves of bookstores and toy shops. The books were sold in numerous countries, and Rowling gained worldwide fame. With this success, she also became a multimillionaire and no longer needed to worry where her next paycheck would come from. By the publication of book seven, Rowling had remarried and had two more children. It was a long way from where she was in 1994—a single mother on state benefits, walking through the streets of Edinburgh and looking for a place to write her book.

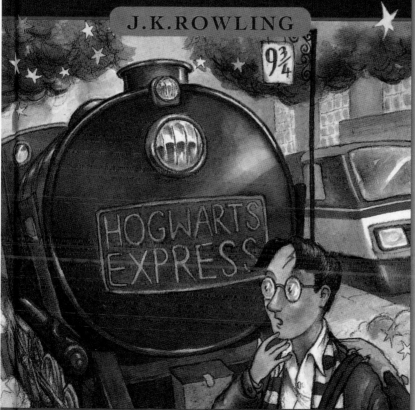

Harry Potter and the Philosopher's Stone *marked the beginning of a worldwide phenomenon surrounding the Harry Potter series.*

Joanne was frequently read to as a child, which may have sparked her lifelong love of reading and writing.

Family Origins

Joanne Rowling was born on July 31, 1965, in Yate, England. A short time later, the Rowling family moved to a house on Nicholls Lane, four miles (6 km) from their previous residence. Many of their new neighbors worked at the Bristol

Factories, as did Joanne's father, Peter. These
factories eventually merged into Rolls-Royce.
Joanne's father continued to work there and was
promoted into management over the course of his
career. A nearby family with the last name of Potter
provided friendship for the Rowling family as well as
inspiration for the last name of Joanne's hero years
later.

THE BIRTH OF A WRITER

Joanne's mother, Anne, stayed home to take care
of Joanne and her sister, Dianne. When Joanne was
five, she began going to school. On the first day,
she donned her school uniform and walked with her
mother to St. Michael's Church of England School.
She went home with her mother for lunch. After
lunch Joanne was confused about having to return
to school. She did not understand that she would go
to school each day, before and after lunch. But once
she understood this, she was happy to attend.

Both parents frequently read to their daughters.
One of Joanne's earliest memories with books is
hearing her father read *The Wind in the Willows*. She also
loved Richard Scarry books with their portrayals
of animals doing human things. Scarry's stories

inspired Joanne to write her first story at the age
of six about a rabbit who had the measles and was
cheered up by a Miss Bee and other friends. Joanne
and her sister really wanted a rabbit of their own,
so Joanne created one with her imagination. She
later said, "Ever since Rabbit and Miss Bee, I have
wanted to be a writer, though I rarely told anyone
so. I was afraid they would tell me I didn't have a
hope."[1] Joanne began to entertain her sister with the
stories she created, and thus began a long history of
amusing friends with storytelling.

Changing Schools

When Joanne was nine, her family moved to
Tutshill, a town on the border between Wales and
England and between two rivers, the Wye and the
Severn. The Rowlings' new home was in a beautiful
setting in the country. Joanne's parents were from
London and had always dreamed of raising their
children away from the city. The cliffs offered
amazing views of the river, and the woods offered
opportunities for adventures for young Joanne
and Dianne.

While Joanne loved the country setting of her new
home, she later said, "The only fly in the ointment

was the fact that I hated my new school."[2] Joanne's life as a student at Tutshill Church of England Primary School began in the fall of 1974. She described the school as "Dickensian," referring to the novels of Charles Dickens set in the mid-nineteenth century of Victorian England.[3] The school had rolltop desks and inkwells that gave students the feeling of stepping back in time to a classroom from long ago.

Joanne's teacher at the school may also have seemed like a character from an unpleasant Dickens novel, except she was not safely contained in the pages of a book. The first thing the teacher did to organize her class was create a seating chart based on her perceived aptitude of her students. She did this using the results of a math test that involved fractions. Unfortunately for Joanne, she had not learned fractions yet. Therefore, she was seated in the row

A Bullying Teacher

Rowling's views on the harm teachers can cause when they bully students is seen through her portrayal of Professor Snape. Within his first moments with a class, Snape insults students by saying, "I can teach you how to bottle fame, brew glory, even stopper death—if you aren't as big a bunch of dunderheads as I usually have to teach."[4]

However, as the series continues, Rowling reveals the complexities of Snape's character. She reveals the bullying to which Snape was subjected by Harry's father. This detail may help readers begin to sympathize with Snape.

on the far right of the class, along with the other students whom the teacher believed lacked potential. The students whom the teacher believed to be the smartest were seated along the left side of the room.

Joanne applied herself in school and eventually was promoted to sit on the left side. As Rowling remembers,

> *I was promoted to second left. But the promotion was at a cost. [My teacher] made me swap seats with my then best friend. So in one short walk across the room I became clever but unpopular.*[5]

Tours Based on the Harry Potter Series

Fans of the Harry Potter series can take organized trips based on the books and movies. Tours have revolved around places in Scotland and England that have influenced the stories and have sometimes corresponded with the release of books and movies. Some tours borrowed ideas from the books such as sending a welcome letter to tourists fashioned after the first letter Harry received welcoming him to Hogwarts.

The memory of this teacher helped Joanne shape one of her characters in the Harry Potter books—Professor Snape, an unpopular teacher among the students at Hogwarts, a school for witches and wizards. Joanne drew upon this time in her life to develop one other character as well—Hermione. She later said,

> *Hermione was very easy to create because she is based on myself at the age of eleven. She is really a caricature of me.*

Like Hermione I was obsessed with achieving academically, but this masked a huge insecurity.[6]

In the midst of moving and adjusting to a new school, Joanne dealt with a tragic loss. Her grandmother died. Joanne and her sister had spent countless hours playing in the grocery store owned by her grandmother Kathleen and her grandfather Ernie. Joanne later honored the memory of her grandmother by taking her name as

Goudge's Influence

Joanne was influenced by author Elizabeth Goudge's descriptions of food. In her first food description in *The Little White Horse*, Goudge writes,

> There was home-made crusty bread, hot onion soup, delicious rabbit stew, baked apples in a silver dish, honey butter the colour of marigolds, a big blue jug of warm mulled claret, and hot roasted chestnuts folded in a napkin.[7]

Rowling's passages about food are similarly as scrumptious as Goudge's, particularly when considering Harry is a child who was never allowed to eat as much as he wanted the first 11 years of his life. His first meal at Hogwarts is described in detail:

> roast beef, roast chicken, pork chops and lamb chops, sausages, bacon and steak, boiled potatoes, roast potatoes, fries, Yorkshire pudding, peas, carrots, gravy, ketchup, and for some strange reason, peppermint humbugs.[8]

Both authors also use humor and detail in their character descriptions. Goudge describes the uncle of the heroine of *The Little White Horse*: "He had a huge white wig like a cauliflower on his head, and his double chins were propped by a cravat of Honiton lace."[9] This description may even sound a bit like Harry's Uncle Vernon.

a middle name and using it as a part of the name that made her famous.

INFLUENTIAL BOOKS

Throughout her childhood, Joanne was a voracious reader. Through her reading, she came across several works that influenced her writing. She has stated that Edith Nesbit's *The Railway Children* and *The Story of the Treasure Seekers* as well as C. S. Lewis's *The Chronicles of Narnia* were literary influences. However, it is Elizabeth Goudge's *The Little White Horse* that she names as one of the most important influences on her conception of Harry Potter. Goudge's book was appreciated not only by Joanne but by the literary world as well. In 1946, it won the Carnegie Medal for children's literature. Part of the reason Joanne liked the book so much was because "the heroine was quite plain."[10] But she also recognized that it was well written. Goudge's attention to describing food in her books influenced Joanne. She once said that Goudge "always included details of what her characters were eating and I remember liking that. You may have noticed that I always list the food being eaten at Hogwarts."[11]

Joanne and Dianne explored the English countryside while growing up in Tutshill.

In high school, Joanne became fluent in English, German, and French and passed difficult tests in the subjects.

Broadening Horizons

As a teenager, Joanne attended a new school, Wyedean Comprehensive School. Eventually, her mother began to work at the school as a laboratory assistant in the chemistry department. So Joanne, Dianne, and their mother again walked to and from school together each morning and afternoon.

Like many secondary school students, the teens at Wyedean Comprehensive tended to divide themselves into groups according to interests. Joanne's friends were usually classified as intelligent and hard-working. Joanne excelled in many languages during her course of study. She took advanced classes in English, German, and French, and passed difficult tests called A-levels in these subjects.

One teacher inspired her as both a person and a writer. Miss Lucy Shepherd was a firm but enthusiastic English teacher who truly seemed to care about her students. Joanne loved English and worked hard in Shepherd's class. She later explained that while Shepherd could be "caustic," she was also "conscientious" and provided Joanne with an "introduction to a different kind of woman. . . . A feminist, and clever."[1] Shepherd taught Joanne how to organize her writing. After the publication of the first Harry

Comprehensive School

A comprehensive school in Britain is the equivalent of a public school in the United States. The quality of the comprehensive schools varies across the country, but students do not pay fees or take exams for admittance. Joanne's school has been described by staff as a mix of students from different economic backgrounds.

Potter book, Rowling received a positive letter from Shepherd. Rowling said it meant more to her than public praise because she knew Shepherd would only write what she truly thought.

BEYOND THE CONFINES OF THE COUNTRY

As Joanne grew older, the river and woods in Tutshill that once enchanted her began losing their charm. She longed to go to movies and the theater and get away from the country. She did have a study abroad experience in France at the age of 13, but she was not assigned to a beautiful place. She found herself in a poor coal town near Lille, which still used outdoor toilets.

In eleventh grade, Joanne saw her first play, William Shakespeare's *King Lear*, in Stratford-upon-Avon, Shakespeare's birthplace. She saw Shakespeare's *The Winter's Tale* as well, which has a character named Hermione, a name she saved for years to give to a character in the Harry Potter books. Joanne enjoyed

---

An Advanced Reader

In addition to *The Little White Horse*, Joanne loved the novels *Black Beauty* and *Little Women*. She said, "I was Jo March for a few months."[2] It was not long before she was reading very advanced books for her age. Joanne was 11 or 12 when she read Jane Austen's *Pride and Prejudice* and 14 when she read William Thackeray's *Vanity Fair*. She said, "I know that sounds precocious but it was there, so I read it."[3]

dancing, but there were few opportunities to do so as a teen. She especially enjoyed the music of The Clash and pretended to play guitar solos.

More Literary Inspiration

Joanne continued to read avidly as she matured. Jane Austen was an important author to Joanne as a teen and has remained important throughout her life. Joanne also read the autobiography *Hons and Rebels* by Jessica Mitford after her great-aunt gave her the book. Mitford, whom she saw as independent and brave, inspired Joanne. The author left home and fought in the civil war in Spain against the wishes of her family. She was a socialist even though she came from a very wealthy family. She believed in education for girls, although her family did not. Joanne especially admired Mitford's commitment to human rights. One of the biggest tributes Joanne has made to the life of Jessica Mitford is by naming her first child, Jessica, after the author.

A Censored Book

There is only one time Joanne remembers her mother censoring what she read. The young Rowling had been given a book based on a TV series called *The Avengers*. Rowling remembers that the beginning of the book was very scary. She said, "I was glad when Mum said—it was the only time she did—that I shouldn't read any more."[4]

Her Mother's Illness

The stability of the Rowling family was challenged when Joanne's mother started having health problems. Anne began experiencing numbness and difficulty with movement and was diagnosed with multiple sclerosis. The disease is difficult to treat, and no cure was offered for Anne, who had a severe form of the disease. The disease affected her central nervous system, causing messages sent from the brain to the nerves to become confused. Her body could not respond normally to the distorted messages. However, the disease's effects were inconsistent. Some days Anne could carry out her typical duties at work and home, and other days she had trouble walking.

Shortly after her diagnosis, Anne quit her job as a laboratory assistant at Wyedean Comprehensive. She was concerned she might break lab samples and hinder her department's work. When she was doing well, Anne would clean the church next door to the Rowlings' home to keep herself occupied while the girls were at school. The family did what they could to support Anne by helping when she was not doing well and gathering as much information as they could about multiple sclerosis.

The Car That Drove Her Imagination

During Joanne's senior year of high school, she made an important friend. Seán Harris moved to the area from Cyprus. Joanne loved to go places with Seán in his turquoise Ford Anglia. She said that the car "spelled freedom. . . . When you live in a village in the country, driving is very important."[5] This model of car has a special role in the Harry Potter books: it is a turquoise Ford Anglia that helps Harry and his friends several times in *Harry Potter and the Chamber of Secrets*. Rowling said, "I couldn't have just any old car rescuing Harry and Ron Weasley to take them back to Hogwarts."[6]

Voldemort and Hitler

Rowling may have had Adolf Hitler in mind when creating the great antagonist of the Harry Potter books, Voldemort. Hitler was the leader of Nazi Germany during World War II (1939–1945). He is recognized as one of the cruelest and most oppressive leaders of the twentieth century due to the scope of devastation caused by his ideologies. Many readers acknowledge the links between Voldemort and Hitler. Both leaders demanded full allegiance from their followers and committed heinous crimes. Both Hitler and Voldemort held deeply racist beliefs. Hitler believed Jews were inferior because of their biology and that Aryans—Caucasians of non-Jewish descent—were superior ethnically and culturally to all other people. Voldemort believed nonmagical people or half bloods (those with both a magical parent and a non-magical parent) were inferior to wizards and witches.

Rowling points more directly at Hitler and World War II when she describes Professor Dumbledore's victory over the dark wizard Grindelwald and his ideology of wizard supremacy.

Perhaps when Joanne was in Seán's car, she felt as if she were flying, too. Rowling has said she is not always conscious of how she inserts herself into her writing:

> *It often isn't until I re-read what I've written that I realize where certain bits of my stories have come from. Harry was rescued by that car, just as the car rescued me from my boredom.*[7]

Rowling gave Ron some of the qualities of her best friend, Seán Harris. She said, "Ron Weasley isn't a living portrait of Seán, but he really is very Seán-ish."[8] Rowling dedicated *Harry Potter and the Chamber of Secrets* to Seán.

*Harry, Hedwig, and Ron (not shown) traveled to school in a Ford Anglia
similar to the one Joanne rode in throughout high school.*

Rowling attended the University of Exeter from 1983 to 1987, earning a bachelor's degree in French and classics.

LEAVING HOME

While she was most often described as quiet and shy as a young girl, Rowling became more social in high school. During her last year at Wyedean, she was voted head girl by her peers and the Wyedean faculty. As head girl, Rowling was

expected to be a role model for other
students and a representative for the
school. She also needed to oversee
other prefects, who are students that
help maintain discipline and order at
school. After competently fulfilling
these roles for a year, she graduated
from Wyedean Comprehensive in
1983.

ON TO EXETER

It is common for British students
to take a year off between high school
and college to pursue things such as
travel and work. However, Rowling
did not choose to do this. She
wanted to continue her education
right away. Rowling applied to
Oxford University, but she was not
accepted. Instead, she was accepted
to the University of Exeter in Devon,
England, and began classes there in
1983. It was a couple of hours from
home—close enough for her family
to visit her, but far enough away

Oxford Rejection Fair?

Some thought Rowling was discriminated against in her application to Oxford because she graduated from a comprehensive school rather than a private one. Her former chemistry teacher, Mr. Nettleship, said another student from a private school was accepted even though her grades were similar to Rowling's. Nettleship said that he believed the other student was favored "because . . . her parents had been able to afford to send her [to school]."[1]

to allow her some distance to grow and change in the formative years of college. She studied French and classics, with an emphasis in Greek and Roman studies. While Rowling liked studying mythology, she was not very inspired by French or her course work in general. Rather than focusing on school with the same intensity as her years at Wyedean, she was known to be a dreamy, average student. She liked to spend time with her friends at the Devonshire House coffee bar, sipping coffee and smoking.

A Secret Dream

Even though Rowling still longed to become a writer, she continued to keep her goal a secret. The idea of studying English at the university was considered impractical by Rowling's parents and others in her community. She was influenced by her parents to study languages. Their argument was that the course of

Another Character Based on Real Life

Rowling based Professor Binns in the Harry Potter series on a boring lecturer from the classics department at Exeter. Professor Binns is a ghost who teaches History of Magic. He died in his sleep one night but woke up to teach the next day and every day thereafter. Binns puts his classes to sleep daily.

study would make it easier to get a practical job as a translator or a bilingual secretary. Instead of flowing into writing, Rowling's creative energy was channeled into storytelling for her friends.

STUDYING ABROAD

While studying French was not her deepest passion, Rowling did love her year abroad in Paris, France, which was a requirement to earn her degree. During her time there, she taught English in a French school part-time and learned to navigate another culture. Once she returned to Exeter, her studies in French allowed

Choice and the Sorting Hat

Many people can relate to the tension Rowling felt when trying to decide a major in college and to find a career as a young adult. This struggle is also portrayed in the magical community of the Harry Potter books as well. From the first day students join Hogwarts, the Sorting Hat shapes their futures. Students are divided among four different houses based on their character, interests, and intelligence. The house the Sorting Hat chooses influences the course of the student's life. Perhaps when Rowling was developing the character of the Sorting Hat, she was thinking about how choosing a major impacts one's future.

But while a student usually gets to select his or her major, the Sorting Hat chooses a student's house. However, in Harry's case, the Sorting Hat listened to Harry's wish. He specifically asked the hat not to put him in the Slytherin house, even though the hat was inclined to do so. This act began Harry's journey to shape his own destiny and the Harry Potter saga.

Sacrifice for Love

Rowling read Charles Dickens's *A Tale of Two Cities* while in France. In the book, Sydney Carton takes the place of Charles Darnay at the guillotine because he loves Darnay's wife. Carton says, "It is a far, far better thing that I do, than I have ever done; it is a far, far better rest that I go to, than I have ever known."[3] Rowling has said that this is "the most perfect last line of a book ever written."[4] The practice of sacrificing oneself for love is paramount in the Harry Potter series. Harry's mother sacrifices for him, as does Snape. And Harry attempts to sacrifice himself to thwart Voldemort. Believing that the only way to destroy Voldemort is through his own death, Harry tries to let Voldemort kill him.

Rowling to use her creativity as a volunteer costume designer for the French play *The Agricultural Cosmonaut* by Obaldia. She continued writing stories at this time and coming up with ideas for future novels. In 1987, Rowling graduated from Exeter.

THE WORST SECRETARY

After graduation, Rowling worked as a temp, or someone who temporarily fills in, at different companies. The main value of this work was that she learned to type quickly, which she appreciated for her writing aspirations. Looking back, Rowling laughs about how unsuited she was for secretarial work because she was so disorganized. She once said, "Me as a secretary? I'd be your worst nightmare."[2] Rowling finally settled on a permanent position at Amnesty International, a human rights organization that works to free wrongly imprisoned people around the world. She firmly believed in the organization's mission and hoped her work as a research assistant could make a difference in the world. She was assigned to the African department, where she researched human rights abuses in African countries whose dominant language is French. Rowling was deeply affected by working at the organization. While at Amnesty International, she read about atrocities committed in African countries, but she also saw the good in humankind through volunteers and co-workers wanting to help strangers in need. She later said,

> Amnesty mobilizes thousands of people who have never been tortured or imprisoned for their beliefs to act on behalf of those who have. The power of human empathy, leading to collective action, saves lives and frees prisoners. Ordinary people, whose personal well-being and security are assured, join together in huge numbers to save people they do not know, and will never meet. My small participation in that process was one of the most humbling and inspiring experiences of my life.[5]

During her breaks and evenings, Rowling went to cafes to write. Sometimes she even wrote during slow periods of work. By the age of 25, she had written two novels, but she never sent them to literary agents or publishers because the writing did not meet her personal standards. It would be several years until Rowling had a book with which she was confident enough to seek publication. ⌐

Rowling studied abroad in Paris while in college.

The idea for Harry Potter came to Rowling while riding on a train in 1990.

FINDING HER CHARACTER

In 1990, one of the biggest life-changing
events in Rowling's life occurred. She was
riding a train from Manchester to London when she
dreamed up the character who would change her life
forever: Harry Potter. Rowling later recalled what

it was like when Harry entered her mind:

> *I have never felt such a huge rush of excitement. I knew immediately that this was going to be such fun to write. I didn't know then that it was going to be a book for children—I just knew that I had this boy, Harry.*[1]

She felt like she had to learn about Harry's life story as though she was not the one creating it; there were mysteries about him. She knew he was a wizard orphan about to go to boarding school, but she did not know why he was an orphan. She also imagined Ron Weasley, Nearly Headless Nick, Hagrid, and Peeves. She did not have a notebook or a working pen, items she typically had with her. Too shy to ask for one, she dreamed about her new characters and their wizarding school, Hogwarts, on the train ride home. Ultimately, she believes it was good

The Importance of Trains

Just as Rowling began a new journey on a train as she envisioned Harry Potter for the first time, so too does Harry begin a new life on a train. In book one, Harry is in awe as he rides the Hogwarts Express to his future school. Yet, riding the Hogwarts Express is not only for Harry Potter characters. Each year, a travel company called HP Fan Trips offers a Harry Potter themed vacation that features a ride in the Hogwarts Express train carriages that are used in the Harry Potter movies.

she had to process the story in her mind first because she was "besieged by a mass of detail, and if it didn't survive that journey, it probably wasn't worth remembering."[2]

LIFE AS INSPIRATION

Rowling's relationship with her mother during this time led to an important aspect of the Harry Potter books. Anne's quality of life had continued to deteriorate since she was diagnosed with multiple sclerosis. When Rowling saw her at Christmas the year before her inspired train ride, she knew her mother looked thin and frail, but did not realize how close she was to the end of her life. Shortly after that visit in December 1990, Rowling's mother died. Everything her mother left her was stolen in a home burglary. Even though Rowling started writing Harry Potter six months before her mother's death, Rowling never mentioned the book to her. It is something she has said she deeply regrets.

Eventually Rowling infused her writing with her longing for her mother and sadness over her death. Rowling created the Mirror of Erised, which appears in *Harry Potter and the Sorcerer's Stone*, as she grappled with her loss. The Mirror of Erised allows viewers to

Rowling imagined Harry with brown disheveled hair, round glasses, and a lightning bolt scar on his forehead. The character would one day be on millions of book covers around the world.

see their deepest desires. Harry saw his parents, who died when he was a baby. When Dumbledore warns Harry that people have languished away in front of the mirror because it prevents them from living life, it is as though the headmaster were speaking to Rowling or anyone else who had lost someone precious.

The period after Anne's death was tremendously difficult for Rowling, and although people were supportive, she simply wanted to escape from everything and everyone around her. She began to consider making a big life change. Remembering how much she enjoyed teaching English in Paris during her college years at Exeter, Rowling thought another job teaching abroad could offer just the kind of change she had in mind.

Understanding Loss

Throughout the Harry Potter books, Rowling convincingly writes of Harry's sense of loss. Rowling knew what this felt like because she had lost her own mother. Upon the dissolution of her marriage, she may have felt a compounded sense of loss knowing her family was broken and that Jessica would grow up without her father.

While Rowling explains that her chapter on the Mirror of Erised in the first book of the Harry Potter series expresses her emotions over the loss of her mother, it also conveys the loss of generations of a family. In the mirror, Harry sees himself standing with his parents and all of his relatives behind them. People who have lost loved ones may understand what compels Harry to repeatedly seek the comfort found in the images in the mirror. When Rowling writes of Dumbledore saying, "This mirror will give us neither knowledge or truth. Men have wasted away before it . . . not knowing if what it shows is real or even possible," she helps her readers, as well as herself, face life and all its wonders instead of pining away over what might have been.[3]

Life in Portugal

In 1991, Rowling found a job teaching English in Porto, Portugal, a city near the mouth of the Rio Douro and the Atlantic Ocean. She lived with two other women, Aine Kiely from Ireland and Jill Prewett from England, who were teaching at Encounter English School with Rowling. There, they taught English to people of various ages. Not only did these women live together, but they also supported one another in their teaching. The three roommates also enjoyed going out dancing. *Harry Potter and the Prisoner of Azkaban* is dedicated to Kiely and Prewitt as a testimony to their importance in Rowling's life.

Rowling taught in the evenings, so she was able to work on her Harry Potter book during the day and on the weekends once her lesson plans were finished. She would write the story in longhand and then type it in

Quidditch

In the Harry Potter series, wizards follow the game of Quidditch with as much enthusiasm as any popular sport in real life. Two teams on broomsticks play against each other in an outdoor stadium. Seven players are on each team: one Keeper, two Beaters, three Chasers, and one Seeker. The game has four balls, one Quaffel, two Bludgers, and one Golden Snitch, which play key roles in the game.

On opposite sides of the field are three ring-shaped goals that are protected by the Keeper. Chasers try to get the Quaffel into one of these rings to score points for their team. Meanwhile, the Beaters of each team try to keep the Bludgers, which fly at random and hit all players, from knocking players off their broomsticks. In the midst of these events, the Seeker has to find and catch the smallest ball, the Golden Snitch, to end the game.

the computer lab at school before work. In addition
to teaching, writing, and going out with her friends,
Rowling also developed her ability to sketch.

Love in Portugal

After living in Portugal for six months, Rowling
met her future husband, a journalist named Jorge
Arantes. Their relationship quickly became serious.
When Rowling became pregnant, they planned to
travel to England to see her family and share their
exciting news. However, a miscarriage prevented the
trip. In 1992, within a year of meeting, Rowling and
Jorge got married. It was a simple service performed
at the civil register office. Rowling's sister, Dianne,
attended the ceremony. The newlyweds did not go
on a honeymoon, and Rowling taught later that
night. In 1993, Rowling and Jorge had a daughter,
whom they named Jessica. Rowling said Jessica's
birth was the happiest moment of her life up to that
point.

Unfortunately, Rowling and Jorge began
arguing often, and each became unhappy within
the marriage. Less than a year after Jessica's birth,
the couple separated. Shortly after the separation,
Rowling left Portugal with Jessica to live near

In Porto, Portugal, Rowling taught English and met and fell in love with her first husband, Jorge Arantes.

Dianne in Edinburgh, Scotland. She brought three completed chapters of Harry Potter with her. In Scotland, Rowling pushed herself to finish the book before her teaching certification course began. She then sent it off to one publisher and one literary agent in 1995. She also finalized her divorce from Jorge.

It was another dark time for Rowling. After her marriage with Jorge was over, she depended on government subsidies to get by. She was clinically

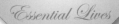

depressed. Around this period, she created another aspect of Harry Potter—the dementors, creatures who sucked the happiness out of their victims. But in the midst of this turmoil, Rowling was about to begin a new chapter of her life.

Rowling created the dementors in Harry Potter
during a dark time in her life.

Rowling was unsure if Harry Potter and the Philosopher's Stone would sell to a publisher.

GETTING PUBLISHED

Rowling sent part of her manuscript to Christopher Little Literary Agency in London. A simple note attached to it stated she included a few chapters of her book and would send the rest if the agency wanted to see it. The book was nearly rejected from the start. The agency did not represent children's books; therefore, the manuscript initially landed in the rejection pile. However, one employee at the agency, Bryony Evans, liked the folder the manuscript was in and perused its contents. She liked Rowling's drawings interspersed in the text, and the story made her laugh. Evans gave it to her boss, Christopher Little, to read quickly before lunch. He too enjoyed it.

A HARD SELL

Despite Evans's and Little's enjoyment of the book, they knew it would be difficult to sell. It was much longer than most books targeted for the nine- to 11-year-old age group that they thought the book would be marketed toward. It also emphasized British culture, which they assumed would be unappealing for the large audience of American

Word Collecting

Rowling has a habit of collecting names and words she loves. For example, she explained, "'Dumbledore' is the Old English word for bumble-bee. I chose it because my image is of this benign wizard, always on the move, humming to himself, and I loved the sound of the word too."[1]

readers to whom the book would likely also be sold. The behavior of the children in the story was also questionable. The three main characters often disobeyed school policies and teachers' orders, which often led them into dangerous situations. Also, the characters attended boarding school, which was assumed to be for especially rich children—children who would probably not appeal to a wider audience. Nonetheless, Little decided to accept Rowling as a client of his agency, and he began searching for publishers who would publish her book.

FINDING A PUBLISHER

The Christopher Little Literary Agency sent the book to nine publishers, all of whom rejected the book with essentially the same critique: the setting and the length were not marketable. But Barry Cunningham, head of a new imprint at Bloomsbury Publishing in London, felt differently about its potential. Cunningham said he was looking for "books children hugged, books they loved, books that made them feel like the author was their best friend."[2] He was not interested in books that focused on issues or problems, which were the kind of books that were popular with teachers and parents at the time. In 1996, he put in an offer to buy the book, but it was pretty low—only £1,500, which was then approximately $2,250. But Rowling was excited nonetheless and accepted the offer. According to Little, Rowling would have sold the book for pennies. Even after her book sold, the publisher and literary agency advised Rowling to continue pursuing work as a teacher because she might never earn enough money to make writing her full-time career.

PAINFUL REVISIONS

Rowling needed to make some changes before publication. Most of the changes were small. But they felt painful to Rowling, who had worked so long and hard on the book. Despite her desire to be published and please those who were making it possible, she refused to make some changes they requested. While she sometimes doubted herself, she believed deeply in the book. Her confidence in Harry Potter came from her commitment to the story.

Awards for Book One

Once *Harry Potter and the Philosopher's Stone* was published, critics around the world recognized it as a special book. The novel received many awards, but two of the most prestigious of these were the Nestlé Smarties Book Prize Gold Award and the British Book Awards Children's Book of the Year.

She did not want to shorten the title, even though the publishers told her it was too long and clunky. She won. Rowling also insisted on keeping the scene in the novel when Ron, Harry, and Hermione fight and defeat the troll in the bathroom. She argued that the scene was essential for character development because it is an important bonding moment for Ron, Harry, and Hermione. Rowling won this argument, too. Rowling's publishers did not want her to use her real name on the book. They were concerned that boys would not read a book written by a woman. They wanted her to use her initials, but Rowling did not have a middle name. Rowling took her grandmother's name, Kathleen, and the pen name—J. K. Rowling—that would bring her fame crystallized.

The Bloomsbury edition of the book was released in 1997. The first printing of 500 copies, which was a normal amount for a writer's first book, did not satisfy the number of customers who wanted to buy *Harry Potter and the Philosopher's Stone*. The book sold out in four days and needed a second printing. The sellout of the first printing was a glimpse into the huge success the series would have.

Scholastic purchased the rights to publish Harry Potter and the Philosopher's Stone *in the United States, and changed the title to* Harry Potter and the Sorcerer's Stone *for the new audience.*

A Book Auction

When a publisher in one country buys a writer's book, the rights to the book can still be sold to another publisher in a different country. This is what happened with Rowling's book. Although it had found a British publisher, Christopher Little was still trying to find an international publisher. He hoped to find a more attractive deal for Rowling, considering the Bloomsbury contract was not a financially lucrative one. Little thought the odds of doing this were good since he was trying to sell the international rights as the book was becoming successful in Great Britain.

Arthur A. Levine, an imprint of the publisher Scholastic in the United States, became interested in purchasing the book rights. The Arthur A. Levine imprint was intended to publish fewer than ten titles a year, and Rowling's *Harry Potter and the Philosopher's Stone* was just the sort of book they were looking for. The enthusiasm from the Bloomsbury staff was what encouraged editors at the Levine imprint to look at the manuscript in the first place. But by that time, several other U.S. publishers were interested in the book as well. An auction was held to determine who would publish it.

The Lord of the Rings and Harry Potter

When asked about the comparisons people were making between J. R. R. Tolkien's *The Lord of the Rings* and her Harry Potter series, Rowling said,

> I think, if you set aside the fact that the books overlap in terms of dragons and wands and wizards, the Harry Potter books are very different, especially in tone. Tolkien created a whole mythology. I don't think anyone could claim I have done that. On the other hand, he didn't have Dudley.[3]

The humorous remark about Dudley does highlight a striking difference between Tolkien's and Rowling's novels. Most readers will not find themselves laughing when reading about Frodo's quest with the ring. The trilogy's tone is dark, grave, and serious. Darkness is an element in Rowling's books, too; however, it is often mitigated with humor.

SCHOLASTIC WINS

When Scholastic won the auction at $105,000, it was the most Scholastic had ever paid for a book. This price was unusually high for the children's book market at the time, especially for an author's first book. Buying Rowling's manuscript was a risk for Scholastic, but one that soon paid off.

Scholastic wanted one large change to the book that Rowling later regretted making. The publisher would change the name from *Harry Potter and the Philosopher's Stone* to *Harry Potter and the Sorcerer's Stone*. Still, Rowling was amazed when she found out the news of the auction. Her first thoughts were that she could buy a house for herself and Jessica in a good neighborhood with a good school. But she was secretly terrified. Her British and American publishers had championed book one. Bloomsbury sent her enough

A Mother's Love

One of Rowling's most important roles in life is being a mother. She loves her children dearly. Love, especially a mother's love, is a significant theme in the Harry Potter books as well. It is the love Harry's mother, Lily, has for Harry that protects him from Voldemort and strips Voldemort of most of his powers. Because Lily's love kept Harry alive, some of Voldemort's power was transferred to Harry, protecting him from harm and equipping him for the ultimate duel between the two of them.

The fact that Voldemort discounts love and its power is what ultimately leads him to his own undoing. It is also what prompts Dumbledore to tell Harry: "Do not pity the dead, Harry. Pity the living, and, above all, those who live without love."[4]

Children of all ages are captivated by the books in the Harry Potter series.

lilies to fill her apartment with their fragrance. But
Rowling was having a hard time writing the second
book in the series, *Harry Potter and the Chamber of Secrets*.
She felt pressure to write something better than the
first book and feared that it would not be as good.

Selling Her Life Story

Because the auction price for Rowling's book was record breaking, people became interested not only in the Harry Potter book but also in the writer who accomplished such a feat. Rowling's agent encouraged her to release her story to reputable news sources, rather than to tabloid journalists or gossip columnists. The story of a single mother living on welfare intrigued people. She did not enjoy the way the story became sensationalized and romanticized, nor did she enjoy the attention from the press:

> *I found the attention just overwhelming, and I had no one to talk to about it—no one. I wasn't with anyone, I wasn't in a relationship at that time. No one I knew personally had ever been through anything like this.*[5]

Rowling would have to balance the success of her books and the interest

Inspiration for Humor

Jane Austen is a writer whom Rowling continues to read for pleasure and inspiration. Like Rowling, Austen also uses humor skillfully to amuse the reader and reveal important aspects of her characters. For example, in *Pride and Prejudice*, the deeper aspects of the relationship between the Bennett parents are suggested by the humor Mr. Bennett uses when talking to his wife. After Mrs. Bennett complains that Mr. Bennett has no compassion for her nerves, he tells her, "You mistake me, my dear. I have a high respect for your nerves. They are my old friends. I have heard you mention them with consideration these twenty years at least."[6]

in her life throughout the rest of the Harry Potter series.

The Seven Harry Potter Books

In the next ten years, the other six Harry Potter books would be published. The seven books in the series are, in order:

- *Harry Potter and the Philosopher's Stone* (*Harry Potter and the Sorcerer's Stone* in the United States)
- *Harry Potter and the Chamber of Secrets*
- *Harry Potter and the Prisoner of Azkaban*
- *Harry Potter and the Goblet of Fire*
- *Harry Potter and the Order of the Phoenix*
- *Harry Potter and the Half-Blood Prince*
- *Harry Potter and the Deathly Hallows*

Rowling signs a copy of Harry Potter and the Sorcerer's Stone *for a young fan.*

Chapter 7

*In 2000, a writing contest allowed Harry Potter fans
to meet and hang out with Rowling.*

FINANCIAL SUCCESS

For a writer who never expected to make much money, Rowling was thrilled with her first royalty check of £800, then approximately $1,200, which came from the British edition of Harry Potter. But it was her book's sale to Scholastic that allowed her to move forward in her desire to buy a house. She wanted to be near her sister and close to a good school for Jessica. Rowling never learned to drive, so it was important for her to be within walking distance of these things. The neighborhood she moved into was near Craiglockhart Primary School in Ashley Terrace, a neighborhood of Edinburgh. The neighborhood was filled with long-term residents who maintained lovely gardens. Rowling and Jessica moved into a two-bedroom house. Soon they added a rabbit, a guinea pig, and a cat to their family.

RECOGNITION

Rowling was not famous enough to be recognized by her neighbors yet. But eventually word spread at Jessica's school that Jessica's mother wrote *Harry Potter and the Philosopher's Stone*. By that time, the book's popularity was growing, and Jessica's classmates began asking her about the book. Yet, Jessica had never read it. Rowling then started reading the books to Jessica and was happy that her daughter liked them. She also gave some readings at the school so that children would not flood Jessica with questions about her mother and the book.

Before moving into her new home, Rowling delivered the second Harry Potter book, *Harry Potter and the Chamber of Secrets*, to her publisher. Then she asked for it back to revise it for six weeks. The book was published in July 1998 and quickly moved to number one on best-seller lists. While Rowling was again surprised by the success of another book, she was happy that, ultimately, she wrote a book of which she was proud.

NEGOTIATING FILM RIGHTS

In October 1998, her fame increased with the announcement of an upcoming film adaptation of *Harry Potter and the Sorcerer's Stone*. Rowling was in support of the film as long as her criteria were met. She wanted the movies to closely follow the content of the books. She also insisted that British actors were used. Having appreciated Warner Bros.' film adaptations of *The Little Princess* and *The Secret Garden*, Rowling felt comfortable working with them, and the company purchased the film rights for *Harry Potter and the Sorcerer's Stone* and *Harry Potter and the Chamber of Secrets*. Rowling found herself collaborating with the film producers and going over drawings of the set to make sure they were in line with her vision of the wizarding

By the summer of 1999, the first three books in the Harry Potter series were published and distributed around the world.

world. She, along with many Harry Potter fans, looked forward to seeing how the film would portray the game of Quidditch.

PUBLICITY APPEARANCES

Meanwhile, the excitement for the books only grew as Rowling wrote her third book in the series, *Harry Potter and the Prisoner of Azkaban*, which was published in July 1999. News about the popularity of the books among adults as well as children delighted Rowling, but she was not happy about the interest in her personal life. She did not enjoy seeing her picture in newspapers and magazines. Attending a publicity event for the third book, she was shocked to see a long line of people waiting to see her. Originally mistaking the line for something else, she asked if there was a sale nearby. She said,

They whisked me in the back entrance and took me upstairs, and when I walked

Harry's Final Choice

The theme of choice that becomes so central from book four to book seven culminates in the choice Harry has to make at the end of book seven. He willingly sacrifices himself to Voldemort hoping that Voldemort will be destroyed in the process. This choice leads him to a realm where he is balancing between life and death. In this place Dumbledore visits Harry, and Harry asks if Dumbledore wants him to return. Dumbledore responds,

I think . . . that if you choose to return, there is a chance that [Voldemort] may be finished for good. I cannot promise it. But I know this Harry, that you have less to fear from returning here than he does. . . . By returning, you may ensure that fewer souls are maimed, fewer families are torn apart. If that seems to you a worthy goal, then we say good-bye for the present.[1]

through the door there was all this screaming and lots of flashbulbs going off. It was the nearest I'll ever come to being a pop star. I was totally speechless; I didn't know what to do with my face. I wanted to look friendly but I have a feeling I looked guilty and shifty. I signed one thousand four hundred books that day.[2]

Unfortunately for Rowling, who only wanted the publicity to subside, her fame continued to grow with the popularity of the books.

AUTHOR IN DEMAND

Bookstores and communities were also caught off guard with the turnout for Rowling's publicity events. Oftentimes, small stores would find they could not accommodate the thousands of people who would arrive to hear Rowling speak or to have their books signed. Sometimes Rowling could not stay to sign everyone's books because she needed to take care of her daughter. This upset some fans. In order to speak to fans in a more efficient fashion, Rowling agreed to appear on shows such as *Rosie O'Donnell Show* and *Today*. But her publishers still needed to create rules to manage the crowds at publicity events, such as only one hardcover book allowed for signing

Long lines of fans besieged Rowling when she appeared for book signings.

and no personalized notes or photos. As much as
Rowling enjoyed meeting and speaking with her fans,
the fame overwhelmed her. Rowling has said that
even though she is thankful for the popularity of the
books, she would exchange some of the money she
has earned for peace and quiet to write.

ALMOST TOO FAMOUS TO WRITE

Writing the fourth book was not easy. In the midst of growing fame, Rowling found it challenging to juggle her responsibilities. Around this time, her ex-husband told his version of their relationship to the press. Rowling was upset by the release of private details about their difficult relationship. However, she persevered and finished *Harry Potter and the Goblet of Fire*.

The Harry Potter books were becoming so popular that the release date for the fourth book, July 8, 2000, garnered much attention. Until that time, such attention was unusual for the release of a children's book. Rowling and her publishers embraced the excitement, conducting many interviews and setting aside large amounts of money to publicize the event. Advance copies were not released, and the prepublished manuscript was hidden in a bank

More Book Awards

Many awards were given to *Harry Potter and the Sorcerer's Stone*. This pattern continued with books two, three, and four, which all earned prestigious awards. Books two and three earned the Nestlé Smarties Book Prize Gold Award. Book two won the British Book Awards Children's Book of the Year. Book three earned the Bram Stoker Award, the Whitbread Children's Book of the Year, and the British Book Awards Author of the Year. Book four was shortlisted for the British Book Awards Children's Book of the Year, but it did not win the Smarties. However, it did win the Hugo Award, *Publisher's Weekly* Best Children's Book of 2000, and Amazon.com Editor's Choice selection for ages nine through twelve. Finally, book four was listed as a Smithsonian Notable Children's Book.

vault. These secretive prepublication actions increased fans' excitement even more.

The Release of Book Four

For the release of *Harry Potter and the Goblet of Fire*, Bloomsbury Publishing had re-created a Platform Nine and Three-Quarters, an element in the books, at King's Cross Station in England. Rowling arrived there in a light blue Ford Anglia, a similar car to the one Harry and Ron rode in to their second year of Hogwarts. Many Harry Potter fans waited at the station to see Rowling, but she was disappointed by the disruption the press caused, preventing her from interacting with fans. She rode away on a train, waving with sadness as she saw crying children who did not get to talk to her or have their book signed.

Most fans agreed that *Harry Potter and the Goblet of Fire* lived up to the hype. The fourth book introduced a theme that Rowling described as central to

A Favorite Character

While a writer may try not to play favorites, Rowling has admitted that Professor Lupin is one of her favorite characters. She said, "He's a damaged person, literally and metaphorically. I think it's important for children to know that adults, too, have their problems, that they struggle. His being a werewolf is really a metaphor for people's reactions to illness and disability."[3]

the remaining three books. Hogwart's headmaster, Albus Dumbledore, tells his students at the end of book four, "You have to make a choice between what is right and what is easy."[4] Rowling said that all the characters would have to make tough choices in the remaining books.

SPLITTING THE BEST-SELLER LIST

By the release of book four, Harry Potter books had dominated the *New York Times* Best-seller List for 80 weeks. At the time, the newspaper only had one fiction best-seller list that combined books for children and adults. However, because of the domination of the Harry Potter series preventing much adult fiction from making the list, the *New York Times* split the list so that children's best sellers would appear on a separate list. While Rowling was sorry to see her books split from the main list, she hoped it would help children's fiction overall.

Harry Potter in Translation

By 2009, the Harry Potter books had been translated into more than 60 languages, including Urdu, Italian, Latin, Arabic, French, Chinese, Polish, German, Norwegian, Finnish, Japanese, Welsh, Turkish, Estonian, and Afrikaans. The Bible is one of the few books that has been translated into more languages.

Regarding translations, Rowling said, "Sometimes I find strange little aberrations. In the Spanish translation Neville Longbottom's toad—which he is always losing—has been translated as a turtle, which surely makes losing it rather more difficult. And there's no mention of water for it to live in."[5]

Also in 2000, Rowling was proud to accept an honorary doctorate from Exeter University. The speech she delivered to the graduating class was noted for its candor. She inspired the audience by telling them to use their privilege to make the world better.

Rowling waved good-bye to fans who did not get her autograph at the release party for Harry Potter and the Goblet of Fire.

In 2001, Rowling met Neil Murray, whom she married
at the end of the year.

THE COMPLETION
OF THE SERIES

In 2001, one of Rowling's friends introduced her to Neil Murray, who had dark hair and round glasses, similar characteristics to Harry Potter. The two got along well, and their relationship quickly moved into romance.

They married on December 26, 2001. The ceremony was held in their home, the Killiechassie House in the Perth county of Scotland, which they purchased two months prior to the wedding. Only close family attended the wedding, including Jessica; Rowling's father and stepmother; Dianne and her husband; and Murray's parents and sister.

Privately positioned on the banks of the River Tay, the couple's almost 150-year-old manor home was the perfect place for an intimate ceremony. Originally, Murray and Rowling planned to marry on the Galapagos Islands, but they abandoned the plan when details about the marriage were leaked to the press. After they were married, the couple also purchased a multimillion dollar home in London. Neil planned to continue his work as an anesthetist and a general practitioner, although he had taken time off to accompany Rowling on a book tour.

It was becoming increasingly difficult for Rowling to lead a private life. Although she had been labeled reclusive, she preferred to describe herself as keeping her life a secret. The release of the first Harry Potter movie during the November before the wedding only increased her time in the public spotlight.

The Films

During the making of the first film, *Harry Potter and the Sorcerer's Stone*, there was concern that the movie would not be successful. Those involved with the movie were unsure if the book would satisfactorily transfer to film, and if the audience would transfer as well. While several famous British actors were in the movie, the three main actors, Daniel Radcliff, who played Harry Potter, Rupert Grint, who played Ron Weasley, and Emma Watson, who played Hermione Granger, were virtually unknown. Would the young, inexperienced actors be good enough?

Any concern over the success of the movies was alleviated when the first movie broke records of sales profits in the United States on opening day. While in theaters, the film grossed nearly $1 billion worldwide. It was eventually

Writing for Herself

Rowling's passion for writing remained after finishing the Harry Potter series. She is thankful that she no longer feels the pressure to make money by writing. However, she said, "I'm sure I'll always write, at least until I lose my marbles. I'm very, very lucky. Because of Harry's success, I don't need to do it financially, nobody's making me. I just need to do it for myself."[1]

Emma Watson, left, Rupert Grint, center, and Daniel Radcliff, right, appear in their Hogwarts clothing. The actors have appeared in all the Harry Potter movies.

nominated for three Academy Awards in 2002—Best Art Direction, Best Costume, and Best Original Score. However, it did not win in any categories.

CONTINUING TO WRITE

With many of the films still to be made, Rowling needed to focus on continuing to write the series. The fifth book, *Harry Potter and the Order of the Phoenix*, was delayed in publication. It was not possible for Rowling to follow her original plan of writing a book a year. Rowling took some much needed time off. She said,

I came up for air and realized that life could be good if I didn't kill myself. The truth was I might have cracked up if I'd committed to writing another book but I wasn't cracking

---

The Harry Potter Films

Each Harry Potter film has become a box-office blockbuster, and most fans have been happy with the film adaptations of the books. As of 2009, the six movies that had reached theaters had made $4.5 billion at the box office, making the movies the top-earning franchise in history. They are also included in lists of the top-grossing movies of all time.

The three actors who played the main characters were the same in each movie, which gave the movies continuity. But director turnover rate was unusually high. There have been four directors in the six movies released. The films' release dates and directors are:

- *Harry Potter and the Sorcerer's Stone* (2001, Chris Columbus)
- *Harry Potter and the Chamber of Secrets* (2002, Chris Columbus)
- *Harry Potter and the Prisoner of Azkaban* (2004, Alfonzo Cuarón)
- *Harry Potter and the Goblet of Fire* (2005, Mike Newell)
- *Harry Potter and the Order of the Phoenix* (2007, David Yates)
- *Harry Potter and the Half-Blood Prince* (2009, David Yates)
- *Harry Potter and the Deathly Hallows* (part one to be released in 2010 and part two to be released in 2011, David Yates)

up, and I certainly didn't have writer's block as was proved by the enormity of the book that followed my break.[2]

It was a busy few months for Rowling. On March 23, 2003, she had her second child, David. Then in June, the fifth Harry Potter book was released. Although it was well received on the whole, some readers were disappointed in their hero, Harry, finding him whiny and angry. This was not the 15-year-old Harry they imagined. But some thought Harry illustrated a realistic portrayal of a teenage boy.

FINISHING THE SERIES

The trend of needing two years to complete a book continued with the final two books in the series. The publication of the sixth book also closely coincided with the birth of a child. Mackenzie was born on January 23, 2005. The release of

A Detailed World

Many elements of Harry's multifaceted magical world cannot be explained as fully as Rowling would like because the books would be too long. One example of this concerns wands. The final destruction of Voldemort hinges on the behavior of wands as much as the wizards, and the instruments have intrigued many readers. Rowling has been asked repeatedly to comment on the details of wand lore that have not been included in the books. She has said,

"Essentially I see wands as being quasi-sentient. . . . They are not exactly animate, but they're close to it, as close to it as you can get in an object, because they carry so much magic. . . . One will expect a certain loyalty from one's wand. So even if you were disarmed while carrying it, even if you lost a fight while carrying it, it has developed an affinity with you that it will not give up easily."[3]

Harry Potter and the Half–Blood Prince came six months later in July. And in 2007 the last book of the series, *Harry Potter and the Deathly Hallows* was published. Rowling completed the book in Balmoral Hotel in Edinburgh, keeping a "Do Not Disturb" sign on the door throughout the process.

To finish the series after so many years of writing and reading was an amazing experience for Rowling, as well as all Harry Potter fans. She said,

> *You cannot imagine what it feels like, after seventeen years, to be finished, both in a good way and in a bad way. It was so much part of my life. Now I know that millions of people feel huge ownership over the world now, and that's a wonderful thing that they do. They simply can't feel it the way I felt it. I know where I was when I wrote every part of those books. . . . Harry really saved me during some bleak moments in my life, so it's been massive saying goodbye.* [4]

Acclaim for Later Books

All the Harry Potter books have had record-breaking sales, and the books have been distributed in more than 200 territories. Later Harry Potter books were also critically acclaimed. Book five received the WH Smith People's Choice Book Awards in the fiction category and was short-listed for the British Book Awards Book of the Year. But book six only won the British Book Awards Book of the Year. Book seven was named an ALA Notable Children's Book and a *New York Times* Notable Book. It also won *Newsweek's* Best Book of the Year.

Fans in cities across the world, such as these in Singapore, held release parties for the final book, Harry Potter and the Deathly Hallows.

The upside for Rowling was she no longer had to sidestep readers and reporters begging for information about the series. Rowling readily admits that the final book, *Harry Potter and the Deathly Hallows*, is her favorite of the series. She said,

> *I hope that, even if it is not yours, you understood, at least, that this was where the story was always leading; it was the ending I had planned for seventeen years, and there was more*

satisfaction than you can probably imagine in finally sharing it with my readers.[5]

After finishing the Harry Potter series, Rowling announced her desire to take a hiatus from writing to spend more time with her family. As a result of the success of the Harry Potter books, Rowling was able to take time off without worrying about financial burdens. No longer did she worry about making ends meet. She also had the ability to take her time in writing future projects, making sure they were of the quality she demanded before publication.

Honors for Rowling

In 2001, Rowling was awarded the Order of the British Empire for her services to children's literature. The following year she became an honorary fellow of the Royal Society of Edinburgh.

Rowling joined fans at the release party for Harry Potter and the Deathly Hallows *at the Natural History Museum in London.*

Members of Christ Community Church in Alamogordo, New Mexico, prepare to burn Harry Potter books and other materials.

CONTROVERSY AND LIFE BEYOND THE BOOKS

The wildly successful Harry Potter books did not come without controversy. Since 1995, Rowling has been among the authors whose books were most challenged in libraries and schools. Children and parents around the world debated whether it was acceptable to read the books. Many fundamentalist Christians argued that the books supported magic and witchcraft, something the Bible warns against as evil. Jewish, Muslim, and nonreligious people critiqued the books as well. Most of the series' religious opponents were concerned that young readers would become attracted to practicing witchcraft and related religions such as Wicca.

Supporters of the books rejected these claims. They said the series portrayed positive values such as loyalty, courage, and sacrifice. Supporters believed that the books were no different than the multitude of other children's books that dealt with magical worlds and characters. A group opposing censorship formed, calling themselves Muggles for Harry Potter. And while many religious leaders decried the books, others defended them and did not think they were evil or led readers down an evil path. The debate continues, even after the sensation caused by the series has mellowed since its completion.

ROWLING TALKS BACK

Rowling has expressed some confusion over the religious-centered censorship of her books. She has pointed out that the books deal with good and evil and positive values. She questions whether these critics have read the books because she thinks they would see these attributes. One thing that bothers Rowling is criticism that comes without knowledge of some of the major themes, characters, and symbols in the books.

She argues that if people censor her books, many other books would have to be censored if the same criteria were applied to them:

If we are going to object to depicting magic in books, then

Harry Potter's Appeal

The webmaster of the fan Web site *The Leaky Cauldron,* Melissa Anelli, has become a public champion of the Harry Potter books and their fans. She explores the effects of the books on their audience in her book *Harry a History: The True Story of a Boy Wizard, His Fans, and Life Inside the Harry Potter Phenomenon.* She explained that despite the wild fame of the books,

Harry Potter has actually been a very intimate phenomenon, the story of small groups of people acting in ways they shouldn't, doing things they usually wouldn't, and making the kind of history that, without Harry, they pretty much couldn't. There's been one woman, a handful of small companies, and one multibillion-dollar corporation—which has, at times, operated like an independent movie studio—at work. They sold things that aren't supposed to sell, at a time when fantasy books weren't supposed to appeal to a generation of people who weren't supposed to care. At almost every step of Harry's early journey, things occurred in ways they shouldn't, confounded expectations, and nearly didn't happen at all.[1]

we are going to have to reject C. S. Lewis. We're going to have to get rid of the Wizard of Oz. . . . [A] lot of classic children's literature is not going to be allowed to survive that, so I'm very opposed to censorship.[2]

One of the main spokespersons urging schools to ban the books was Laura Mallory, a mom from Georgia who had never read the series. She believed the books would encourage children to practice witchcraft. Rowling said she proposed discussion of the books rather than a ban:

The view I would take in my own life would be to say to my children, "Let's discuss it, let's talk about it honestly." I'm not going to lock away a popular children's book and tell you it's evil. That's nonsense, and I would go further to say that it's damaging. Fundamentalism in any form, in any religion, is intolerant, and tolerance is the only way forward.[3]

In 2005, Mallory began a campaign to ban the Harry Potter books in Gwinnett County, Georgia. When the school board voted against it, Mallory appealed the decision to Georgia's Superior Court. In 2007, the Superior Court also ruled against Mallory.

An attorney holds Harry Potter and the Sorcerer's Stone, *which was reinstated in the school library by a court ruling.*

Are the Books Too Dark?

Opponents of the books were not always driven by religious ideals. Nonreligious people opposed the series, too. They were concerned about the dark aspects of the plot. Voldemort is the terrible antagonist in the series. By contemporary society's standards, he would likely be considered very malevolent. In the first three books of the series, he is a disembodied force, but he is limited in his capacity to harm others. However, by the end of the fourth book, he returns in full-body form and murders a Hogwarts student.

Some people do not think children should be exposed to murder, racism, and genocide, for which Voldemort and his followers are striving. Voldemort wants to cleanse the wizarding community of all those who are muggles, or nonmagical humans. Therefore, he tortures and murders muggles and those who support them. His actions highlight evils from actual human experiences such as racism, and are synonymous with ethnic cleansing.

Supporters of the books do not think the series is too dark and have emphasized the importance of imaginative play in helping children deal with difficult issues and in developing more mature ethical sensibilities. Yet, many supporters also encourage parents and children to talk about the ideas and their cultural implications, a practice Rowling herself recommends.

ARE THE BOOKS WELL WRITTEN?

The quality of the writing in the Harry Potter books has also been debated. While Rowling has

"There are not many writers who have JK's Dickensian ability to make us turn the pages, to weep—openly, with tears splashing—and a few pages later to laugh, at invariably good jokes. The sneerers who hate Harry Potter, or consider themselves superior to those books, often seem to be hating their harm-lessness—the fact that they celebrate happy mid-dle-class family life, and the adventures of chil-dren privileged enough to attend a boarding school. But, as WH Auden said in another context, why spit on your luck? We have lived though a decade in which we have followed the publication of the liveliest, funniest, scariest, and most moving chil-dren's stories ever written. Thank you, JK Rowling."[4]

—*A. N. Wilson,*
in a review of
Harry Potter and
the Deathly Hallows

always said she has tried to write the best books she possibly can, some critics argue that the stories are not artistic enough and that they follow patterns similar to those in other fantasy books. Supporters point out that the books explore age-old ideas and themes that are found in many classic works of literature. In each book, Harry faces challenges similar to those of mythic heroes, who typically experience a series of trials that lead to reorganizations of their worlds. In book one, Harry and his friends pass through each of the protective trials set up by his professors to guard the Sorcerer's Stone. But Harry's ultimate test in the first book is facing Voldemort and winning. All the school finds out about it and rejoices in Harry's victory. Supporters of the books point out that the Harry Potter series explores universal themes that have appealed to readers throughout the ages, and that Rowling's imagination revisits them with a new magical world and characters.

PREJUDICE AND SEXISM IN HARRY POTTER

Some critics have found prejudice and sexism in the Harry Potter books. They have pointed out that non-human creatures such as goblins, house-elves, centaurs, giants, and other magical creatures are sometimes depicted in a demeaning way. Rowling disagrees and has said,

> *The Potter books . . . are a prolonged argument for tolerance, a prolonged plea for an end to bigotry, and I think it's one of the reasons that some people don't like the books.*[5]

Some critics have said that female characters in the story only reinforce gender stereotypes, such as Hermione being studious and rule abiding and Mrs. Weasley being a

Stereotypical Roles?

One critic of the Harry Potter series wrote that the books emphasize traditional roles of gender and race, and the characters that do not fit traditional roles are marginal. While many of the Hogwarts students and teachers are Caucasian, it is necessary to recognize that many other significant characters are of varying magical versions of race: Hagrid is part-giant; Professor Lupin is a werewolf; Dobby is a house-elf; and Firenze is a centaur. Hermione is of nonmagical descent, which some wizards discriminate against. All of these characters play more than marginal roles in the books.

homemaker. But these characters also act and speak out in significant ways. They are not subordinate to the men in their lives, and they do not seem to be disadvantaged by their gender. Hermione often gets Harry, Ron, and herself out of harm's way by using her intelligence and wizarding skill. In book seven, Mrs. Weasley displays her powerful skills as a witch when she battles and kills the powerful, evil witch Bellatrix.

ROWLING ON TRIAL

Criticism about the quality of writing in the series and the acceptability of the books to children were not the only hardships Rowling faced after publication. Several court cases developed around the rights of the Harry Potter material. Charges of plagiarism have been made against Rowling. Nancy Stouffer sued Rowling, claiming the Harry Potter books were based on her work *The Legend of Rah and the Muggles*. The courts ruled in Rowling's favor in 2002. In turn, Rowling has also made charges of plagiarism against others, suing for unauthorized sequels that were published in Chinese. Again, the courts ruled in favor of Rowling.

Rowling arrived at court to testify in a plagiarism case she brought against a Harry Potter lexicon that was being developed.

A long court battle over the rights to Harry Potter material centered on a Harry Potter lexicon that was being developed by Steve Vander Ark. After a court ruling against him and his publisher, Vander Ark shortened some lexicon entries and changed some of the language of his book so it relied less on Rowling's unique writing style. The published version of *The Lexicon: An Unauthorized Guide to Harry Potter Fiction and Related Materials* is an alphabetized guide to characters, terms, and ideas from the books.

Beyond the Seven Books

Rowling also has been active outside the Harry Potter world she created. Humanitarian work has been important to Rowling since she was young. After becoming financially stable, Rowling gave to Amnesty International, where she once worked. Her mother's struggle with multiple sclerosis led Rowling to contribute to others who struggle with the disease. She opened the Stuart Resource Centre for Scotland's Multiple Sclerosis Society and has been involved in several other organizations committed to researching and treating the disease. Her own struggle as a single parent also influenced her charitable contributions. She participates in the National Council for One Parent Families. While she is no longer a member of a one-parent family, she remembers well the difficulties that come with parenting alone.

Since completing the Harry Potter series, Rowling has used her writing to support charities of interest. Rowling wrote *Fantastic Beasts and Where to Find Them* and *Quidditch Through the Ages*. Both books excited Harry Potter fans because they were actual textbooks the Harry Potter characters used in their classes at Hogwarts. She donated the proceeds from these books to Comic Relief, an organization focused on helping poor children in economically struggling countries. Later she published the childhood storybook *Tales of Beedle the Bard*, which is referenced in book seven. Just as Harry and Hermione were curious about all three books because they were raised by nonmagical people, so too were Potter fans happy to have additional glimpses into the wizarding world. The net proceeds from sales of *Tales of Beedle the Bard* are donated to the charity The Children's High Level Group, which

Still a Reader

When asked how she finds time to read in the midst of her busy life, Rowling said, "I read when I'm drying my hair. I read in the bath. I read when I'm sitting in the bathroom. Pretty much anywhere I can do the job one-handed, I read."[6]

was founded by Rowling and Baroness Nicholson of Winterbourne to improve the lives of children who live in institutions.

In an interview shortly after the release of the final Harry Potter book, Rowling mentioned she is likely to write an encyclopedia that would expand on the wizarding world she created for the series. Fans worldwide are waiting expectantly for that day. While Rowling is unsure if she will continue writing books pertaining to Harry Potter after that, she hopes to keep writing for many years.

An active participant in the National Council for One Parent Families,
Rowling attended the organization's national conference in 2001.

TIMELINE

1965	1974	1983
Joanne Rowling is born on July 31 in Yate, England.	The Rowlings move to Tutshill, England, where Joanne attends primary school.	Joanne graduates from Wyedean Comprehensive School.

1992	1993	1995
Rowling marries Jorge Arantes.	Rowling's daughter Jessica is born.	Rowling finishes writing *Harry Potter and the Philosopher's Stone.*

1987	1987	1991
Joanne Rowling graduates from the University of Exeter with a degree in French and classics.	Rowling moves to London to work at Amnesty International as a secretary.	Rowling moves to Porto, Portugal, to teach English.

1995	1997	1998
Rowling gets divorced from Jorge.	*Harry Potter and the Philosopher's Stone* is released in the United Kingdom on June 30.	*Harry Potter and the Chamber of Secrets* is released in the United Kingdom on July 2.

TIMELINE

1999	2000	2001
Harry Potter and the Prisoner of Azkaban is published on July 8.	*Harry Potter and the Goblet of Fire* is published on July 8.	The film version of *Harry Potter and the Sorcerer's Stone* is released by Warner Bros.

2003	2004	2005
Rowling's son, David, is born.	Warner Bros. releases the film version of *Harry Potter and the Prisoner of Azkaban.*	*Harry Potter and the Half-Blood Prince* is published on July 16. Warner Bros. releases the film version of *Harry Potter and the Goblet of Fire.*

2001

Rowling marries Neil Murray.

2002

Warner Bros. releases the film version of *Harry Potter and the Chamber of Secrets.*

2003

Harry Potter and the Order of the Phoenix is published on June 21.

2005

Rowling's daughter Mackenzie is born.

2007

Harry Potter and the Deathly Hallows is published on July 21. Warner Bros. releases the film version of *Harry Potter and the Order of the Phoenix.*

2009

Warner Bros. releases the film version of *Harry Potter and the Half-Blood Prince.*

ESSENTIAL FACTS

DATE OF BIRTH

July 31, 1965

PLACE OF BIRTH

Yate, England

PARENTS

Peter and Anne Rowling

EDUCATION

Tutshill Church of England Primary School, Wyedean
Comprehensive School, University of Exeter

MARRIAGE

Jorge Arantes (October 16, 1992–June 26, 1995)
Neil Murray (December 26, 2001)

CHILDREN

Jessica (1993), David (2003), Mackenzie (2005)

Career Highlights

Rowling wrote the seven-book Harry Potter series that has become a worldwide sensation and one of the best-selling series of all time.

Societal Contribution

Rowling's Harry Potter books have inspired millions of young people and adults to read. She cofounded The Children's High Level Group, an organization that helps children who live in institutions. Rowling also actively supports multiple sclerosis research and opened the Resource Centre for Scotland's Multiple Sclerosis Society.

Conflicts

Rowling struggled with depression and poverty while she was a single mother. Critics of the Harry Potter books have attempted to ban them for a variety of reasons, including that the content is immoral and condones witchcraft.

Quote

"I'm sure I'll always write, at least until I lose my marbles. I'm very, very lucky. Because of Harry's success, I don't need to do it financially, nobody's making me. I just need to do it for myself."
—*J. K. Rowling*

ADDITIONAL RESOURCES

SELECT BIBLIOGRAPHY

Anelli, Melissa. *Harry a History: The True Story of a Boy Wizard, His Fans, and Life Inside the Harry Potter Phenomenon*. New York, NY: Pocket Books, 2008.

Bridger, Francis. *A Charmed Life: The Spirituality of Potterworld*. New York, NY: Image Books, 2002.

Bryfonski, Dedria, ed. *Political Issues in J. K. Rowling's Harry Potter Series*. Detroit, MI: Gale, 2009.

Heilman, Elizabeth E., ed. *Harry Potter's World: Multidisciplinary Critical Perspectives*. New York, NY: Routledge, 2003.

Kirk, Connie Ann. *J. K. Rowling: A Biography*. Westport, CT: Greenwood Press, 2003.

Smith, Sean. *J. K. Rowling: A Biography*. London, UK: Michael O'Mara Books, 2001.

FURTHER READING

Fraser, Lindsey. *Conversations with J. K. Rowling*. New York, NY: Scholastic, 2000.

Sexton, Colleen A. *J. K. Rowling*. Minneapolis, MN: Twenty-First Century Books, 2008.

Steffens, Bradley. *J. K. Rowling*. San Diego, CA: Lucent Books, 2002.

Vander Ark, Steve. *The Lexicon: An Unauthorized Guide to Harry Potter Fiction and Related Materials*. Muskegon, MI: RDR Books, 2009.

WEB LINKS

To learn more about J. K. Rowling, visit ABDO Publishing
Company online at **www.abdopublishing.com**. Web sites about
J. K. Rowling are featured on our Book Links page. These links
are routinely monitored and updated to provide the most current
information available.

PLACES TO VISIT

The Forest of Dean
www.visitforestofdean.co.uk/
Travel to the first national forest park, and enjoy the beautiful
landscape where Joanne spent much of her childhood.

The Harry Potter Exhibition
www.harrypotterexhibition.com/
This traveling exhibit visits science museums all over the country
and focuses on the intersection between science and the Harry
Potter films.

The Wizarding World of Harry Potter
www.universalorlandoresort.com/harrypotter/
Universal Studios, Orlando, FL
At the Wizarding World of Harry Potter, some of the most
treasured aspects of the Harry Potter books come to life.
Visitors can explore Hogwarts castle and Hogsmeade, including
Ollivander's wand shop and Honeydukes.

GLOSSARY

fundamentalism
> The belief that narrowly defined religious rules should be strictly followed.

genocide
> Purposefully seeking to destroy a population of people grouped according to race, ethnicity, or nationality.

headmaster
> The principal of a school.

honorary doctorate
> A doctorate that is awarded by a university to honor someone for his or her work done outside the university.

humanitarian
> Promoting social justice and human welfare.

imprint
> The brand name under which a book publisher releases books.

lexicon
> Dictionary.

manuscript
> A typed document that is submitted for publication.

muggle
> A person without any magical ability.

multiple sclerosis
> A disease that affects the nervous system and can result in paralysis.

mythology
> The study of gods, heroes, and other legendary myths.

plagiarism
> The act of passing off another person's ideas or work as one's own.

prefect
> A student monitor in a school.

racism
> The belief that differences in race produce an inherent superiority or inferiority of a particular race.

royalty
> The share in profits an author receives from his or her book.

SOURCE NOTES

Chapter 1. Writing the First Book
1. Bill Adler, ed. *Kids' Letters to Harry Potter from Around the World*. New York, NY: Carroll & Graf, 2001. 2.
2. Lindsey Fraser. *Conversations with J. K. Rowling*. New York, NY: Scholastic, 2000. 40.
3. Bill Adler, ed. *Kids' Letters to Harry Potter from Around the World*. New York, NY: Carroll & Graf, 2001. 12.

Chapter 2. Family Origins
1. Dedria Bryfonski, ed. *Political Issues in J. K. Rowling's Harry Potter Series*. Detroit, MI: Gale, 2009. 21.
2. Ibid. 22.
3. Lindsey Fraser. *Conversations with J. K. Rowling* New York: Scholastic, 2000.17.
4. J. K. Rowling. *Harry Potter and the Sorcerer's Stone*. New York, NY: Scholastic, 1997. 137.
5. Sean Smith. *J. K. Rowling: A Biography*. London, UK: Michael O'Mara, 2001. 37.
6. Ibid. 45.
7. Elizabeth Goudge. *The Little White Horse*. Cutchogue, NY: Buccaneer Books, 1976. 27.
8. J. K. Rowling. *Harry Potter and the Sorcerer's Stone*. New York, NY: Scholastic, 1997. 123.
9. Elizabeth Goudge. *The Little White Horse*. Cutchogue, NY: Buccaneer Books, 1976. 17.
10. Lindsey Fraser. *Conversations with J. K. Rowling*. New York, NY: Scholastic, 2000. 24.
11. Ibid. 25.

Chapter 3. Broadening Horizons
1. Lindsey Fraser. *Conversations with J. K. Rowling*. New York, NY: Scholastic, 2000. 18.
2. Ibid. 24.
3. Ibid. 25.
4. Ibid.
5. Ibid. 20.
6. Ibid.
7. Ibid.
8. Ibid.

Chapter 4. Leaving Home
1. Sean Smith. *J. K. Rowling: A Biography*. London, UK: Michael O'Mara, 2001. 76.
2. Lindsey Fraser. *Conversations with J. K. Rowling*. New York, NY: Scholastic, 2000. 35.
3. Charles Dickens. *A Tale of Two Cities*. New York, NY: Signet, 2007.
4. Sean Smith. *J. K. Rowling: A Biography*. London, UK: Michael O'Mara, 2001. 88.
5. J. K. Rowling. "Magic for Muggles." *Greater Good Magazine Online*. June 2008. 16 Dec. 2009 <http://greatergood.berkeley.edu/greatergood/2008summer/Rowling149.html>.

Chapter 5. Finding Her Character
1. Lindsey Fraser. *Conversations with J. K. Rowling*. New York, NY: Scholastic, 2000. 37.
2. Ibid. 38.
3. J. K Rowling. *Harry Potter and the Sorcerer's Stone*. New York, NY: Scholastic, 1997. 213.

Chapter 6. Getting Published
1. Lindsey Fraser. *Conversations with J. K. Rowling*. New York, NY: Scholastic, 2000. 55.
2. Melissa Anelli. *Harry a History: The True Story of a Boy Wizard, His Fans, and Life Inside the Harry Potter Phenomenon*. New York, NY: Pocket Books, 2008. 45.
3. Sean Smith. *J. K. Rowling: A Biography*. London, UK: Michael O'Mara, 2001. 92.
4. J. K Rowling. *Harry Potter and the Deathly Hallows*. New York, NY: Scholastic, 2007. 722.
5. Melissa Anelli. *Harry A History: The True Story of a Boy Wizard, His Fans, and Life Inside the Harry Potter Phenomenon*. New York, NY: Pocket Books, 2008. 56.
6. Jane Austen. *Pride and Prejudice*. New York, NY: Pocket Books. 2004. 6.

Chapter 7. Financial Success
1. J. K Rowling. *Harry Potter and the Deathly Hallows*. New York, NY: Scholastic, 2007. 722.
2. Lindsey Fraser. *Conversations with J. K. Rowling*. New York, NY: Scholastic, 2000. 53.
3. Ibid. 40.
4. Anna Weinberg. "Unfogging the Future: What to Look for in the Next Harry Potter." *Book* (May–June 2003): 38. *Literature Resource Center*.

Source Notes Continued

Gale. Hennepin County Library. 7 Aug. 2009. <http://galegroup.com. ezproxy.hclib.org>.
5. Lindsey Fraser. *Conversations with J. K. Rowling*. New York, NY: Scholastic, 2000. 54.

Chapter 8. The Completion of the Series
1. Lindsey Fraser. *Conversations with J. K. Rowling*. New York, NY: Scholastic, 2000. 56.
2. Melissa Anelli. *Harry a History: The True Story of a Boy Wizard, His Fans, and Life Inside the Harry Potter Phenomenon*. New York, NY: Pocket Books, 2008. 150-1.
3. J. K. Rowling. Interview with Melissa Anelli, Sue Upton, and John Noe. "Pottercast 131: J. K. Rowling Interview Transcript." *The Leaky Cauldron*. 23 Dec. 2007. 21 July 2009 <http://www.the-leaky-cauldron. org/2008/1/2/pottercast-131-j-k-rowling-interview-transcript>.
4. Ibid.
5. "J. K. Rowling Updates Website with New Information on ITV Documentary, Events in 'Deathly Hallows,' and More." *The Leaky Cauldron*. 7 Dec. 2007. 18 Nov. 2009 <http://www.the-leaky-cauldron. org/2007/12/7/j-k-rowling-updates-website-with-new-information-on-elder-wand-and-more>.

Chapter 9. Controversy and Life beyond the Books
1. Melissa Anelli. *Harry a History: The True Story of a Boy Wizard, His Fans, and Life Inside the Harry Potter Phenomenon*. New York, NY: Pocket Books, 2008. 19.
2. J. K. Rowling. Interview with Larry King. *Larry King Live*. CNN. 20 Oct. 2000. 16 Jul. 2009 <http://www.cnn.com/ TRANSCRIPTS/0010/20/lkl.00.html>.
3. Melissa Anelli. *Harry a History: The True Story of a Boy Wizard, His Fans, and Life Inside the Harry Potter Phenomenon*. New York, NY: Pocket Books, 2008. 200.
4. A.N. Wilson. Review of *Harry Potter and the Deathly Hallows*, by J. K. Rowling. *Times Online*. 29 Jul. 2007. 1 Oct. 2009 <http://entertainment.timesonline.co.uk/tol/arts_and_entertainment/ books/children/article2139573.ece>.
5. Dedria Bryfonski, ed. *Political Issues in J. K. Rowling's Harry Potter Series*. Detroit, MI: Gale, 2009. 12-13.
6. Lindsey Fraser. *Conversations with J. K. Rowling*. New York, NY: Scholastic, 2000. 87-8.

INDEX

INDEX CONTINUED

ABOUT THE AUTHOR

Victoria Peterson-Hilleque is a freelance writer who lives and works in Minneapolis, Minnesota. She has a master's degree in English literature from the University of St. Thomas in St. Paul, Minnesota. She has taught composition at local universities for several years and is currently working toward an MFA in creative writing at Hamline University, also in St. Paul.

PHOTO CREDITS